Addressing and Resolving Poor Performance

A Guide for Supervisors

**United States
Office Of
Personnel
Management**

Office of Workforce Relations

Table of Contents

Introduction

What Is the Purpose of This Booklet?

Most Federal employees work hard, and their performance is considered good or even exceptional. However, at times Federal supervisors are faced with employees whose performance is not acceptable. The purpose of this booklet is to help you address and resolve poor performance. This guidance should be used in concert with the technical advice you receive from your agency's human resources staff. You should also be aware that most agencies have specific procedures and requirements that must be followed, whether they are part of a negotiated bargaining agreement or other internal agency regulation.

How Should I Use This Booklet?

Addressing and resolving poor performance is a three-step process. These three steps are:

STEP
1

COMMUNICATING EXPECTATIONS AND
PERFORMANCE PROBLEMS

STEP
2

PROVIDING AN OPPORTUNITY TO IMPROVE

STEP
3

TAKING ACTION

This booklet is organized accordingly into three steps. At the end of each section, you will find a checklist as well as answers to commonly asked questions. In the appendix, you will find samples of documents that can be used throughout this process.

INTRODUCTION

Why Should I Address Poor Performance?

Dealing with performance problems is a real challenge for any supervisor. Experienced supervisors often say it is one of the toughest parts of their jobs. Nevertheless, it is a key supervisory responsibility, and failure to address poor performance can have a greater impact than you may appreciate. Let's briefly discuss some of the reasons supervisors often give for not addressing poor performance.

Dealing with poor performance can be time consuming. My time is better spent supervising my productive employees.

While dealing with poor performance can be time consuming, failing to address poor performance sends a clear message to other employees that you have unique standards for poor performers and that they need not meet your performance expectations. With staff cutbacks, it is critical that all employees produce, and ignoring poor performance by some staff can no longer be tolerated. Poor performance usually only gets worse over time—rarely does it correct itself without action on the part of the supervisor.

If I take action against one employee, it will lower morale among other employees and create a less productive work environment.

Actually, taking such action can have just the opposite effect. Most employees want and expect to be held accountable for their work and resent it when others do not "pull their weight." Building a productive team can begin by setting clear expectations and addressing failure to meet those expectations.

Telling employees that they are not performing satisfactorily is unpleasant and requires special human relations skills.

Thankfully, very few individuals enjoy criticizing others. But as a result, most employees receive little or no negative feedback from their supervisors. Constructive counseling given early and regularly not only often leads to performance improvement but also eliminates the need to consider more formal action that is even more unpleasant. Providing such counseling does not require special skills. There are several points to remember, however, and they will be discussed in the next section.

INTRODUCTION

The procedural steps involved in addressing poor performance are complex and highly technical.

Many performance problems can be addressed prior to undertaking any formal action. Furthermore, the procedural steps are actually fairly straightforward and not that complicated. Those steps will be described later in this booklet.

If I do take a formal performance-based action, it is likely to be appealed and ultimately overturned.

Most performance-based actions are not appealed and, when they are, the overwhelming majority are sustained upon appeal to the Merit Systems Protection Board.

Upper management will not support me if I do take action to address poor performance.

The same reasons it makes sense for you to address poor performance should make sense to your supervisor. Share this booklet with your supervisor!

INTRODUCTION

What Can I Do To Prevent Poor Performance?

The focus of this booklet is on helping you address and resolve poor performance. The best way for supervisors to handle poor performance issues is to take action to avoid performance problems before they occur. Such preventive actions include:

• **Communicating clear performance standards and expectations to employees.** **(Consider sharing your supervisor's performance expectations with your staff.)**

If your employees don't understand what is expected, it will be very hard, if not impossible, for them to meet those expectations. Providing clear expectations doesn't necessarily require you to lay out precisely written, detailed instructions on every performance component. Generally, the question you should ask yourself is: "Would a reasonable person understand what was expected?"

• **Providing regular and frequent feedback on performance.**

Such feedback, both positive and negative, whether given in regularly scheduled meetings or in unscheduled discussions, is crucial to ensuring that expectations are understood. Frequent feedback lessens the likelihood that an employee will be surprised if it becomes necessary to take formal steps to resolve poor performance. Always look for opportunities to confirm that your employees understand what is expected.

• **Rewarding and recognizing good performance, informally and formally.**

Recognizing good performance is simply another way of clarifying expectations.

• **Making full use of the probationary period for new employees.**

The importance of the probationary or trial period is discussed in more detail under the "Special Topics" section of this booklet. Performance problems often first show up during the initial period of Government employment. This period is designed to provide an opportunity for management to address such problems. Furthermore, an employee who is terminated during this period is not entitled to most of the procedures and appeal rights granted to employees who have completed probationary/trial periods.

A recurring theme in successful resolution of performance problems is that taking action early is always better than waiting. This statement is definitely true when considering ways to prevent performance problems. Early communication, early feedback (positive and negative), and if appropriate, early termination during a probationary or trial period are all good ways to prevent future performance problems. Investing time early is always time well spent.

STEP

1

COMMUNICATING EXPECTATIONS AND PERFORMANCE PROBLEMS

STEP ONE: COMMUNICATING EXPECTATIONS AND PERFORMANCE PROBLEMS

Why Counsel an Employee?

Most performance problems can be resolved through effective communication between supervisors and their employees. A counseling session is an opportunity to clarify expectations and discuss performance problems. This step will provide advice on preparing for and conducting counseling sessions.

What's the Difference Between Poor Performance and Misconduct?

It is important that you first make sure you are faced with poor performance rather than misconduct. The difference between poor performance and misconduct is explained below.

> Misconduct is generally a failure to follow a workplace rule (whether written or unwritten). Examples of misconduct include tardiness and absenteeism, insubordination, and falsification. Poor performance, on the other hand, is simply the failure of an employee to do the job at an acceptable level. The acceptable level is usually, but not always, documented in written performance standards and is typically defined in terms of quality, quantity, or timeliness. Although it is normal for performance and misconduct to be interrelated, it is important to recognize the difference between the two. **The guidance in this booklet is designed to help you address and resolve problems that are primarily performance based rather than misconduct related.**

How Can I Effectively Counsel an Employee?

If, despite the preventive steps you have taken to avoid poor performance, you find an employee's performance is not meeting expectations, the best approach is to meet with the employee to discuss the performance problem. The focus of this discussion should be to tell the employee exactly what must be done to bring performance up to an acceptable level, both by providing specific examples of poor performance and also suggesting ways that performance can be improved.

It is critical that you review the employee's standards to ensure that they clearly convey what needs to be done in the job. Your human resources staff can assist you in this review. Be sure to ask the employee if he or she understands precisely what must be done to bring performance to an acceptable level.

Immediately after any such discussion with an employee, you should take a few minutes and make a dated note for the file to document the matters discussed and any assistance offered. If such a note would help confirm your mutual understanding of the matters discussed, you should share it with the employee.

At times, you will need the assistance of the Employee Assistance Program (EAP) that is available to provide counseling for physical or mental conditions, or other personal problems. It's a smart idea to know the name of the EAP specialist in your organization and to make sure you understand the services offered through the EAP and how to refer an employee. By doing so, you are prepared to respond if employees raise personal problems that are impacting their work.

Topics Discussed During Counseling Session

✓ Your Expectations

✓ The Employee's Performance Standards

✓ Critical Element(s) Where the Employee Is Failing

✓ What the Employee Must Do To Bring Performance to an Acceptable Level

Effective Counseling Tips

• Before counseling, make sure you can state clearly what would constitute acceptable performance.

• Whenever possible, conduct the counseling session in a private place.

• Arrange adequate time for your comments as well as comments from the employee.

• Clearly state performance expectations and seek confirmation that the employee understands those expectations.

• Focus on the poor performance, not on personalities or other distractions.

• Always maintain a constructive tone, along with a calm and professional demeanor.

• Seek cooperation, NOT confrontation.

• Remember that your goal is to improve the employee's performance, not to win an argument with the employee.

• Try to end the session on a positive note by emphasizing that your mutual goal is improving the employee's performance.

Note: A more detailed discussion on how to prepare for and conduct a counseling session is provided at the end of this section.

Use the following checklist to make sure that you have completed all the actions related to Step One.

Step One Checklist	Yes	No
Are you sure the issue is primarily a performance problem (as opposed to misconduct)?	❏	❏
Have you communicated performance standards to the employee?	❏	❏
Are the standards clear and reasonable?	❏	❏
Have you asked the human resources staff to review the standards for any possible problems?	❏	❏
Have you told the employee what critical elements he or she is failing?	❏	❏
Have you counseled the employee on how to improve to an acceptable level?	❏	❏
Let the employee know if performance is improving or not!		

Step One Questions and Answers

Question: Do I have the authority to tell an employee that his or her performance is unacceptable?

Answer: Yes. More than that, as the employee's supervisor and "rating official," it should be your goal to keep an employee informed about your assessment of his or her performance, particularly when that assessment is negative. Within your agency, there may be a policy or practice you must follow when you notify an employee that his or her performance has become unacceptable. You should contact your human resources office for further information.

Question: Do I have to wait for the annual performance appraisal to tell an employee that his or her performance is unacceptable?

Answer: No, you should not wait. In fact, good managers provide their employees with performance feedback throughout the appraisal cycle. The Office of Personnel Management reinforces this in its regulations where it states that employees need to be notified of unacceptable performance, "At any time during the performance appraisal cycle that an employee's performance is determined to be unacceptable . . ." Notice also that the Governmentwide regulations only call for a determination, not a formal rating of record. Check with your agency on your internal policy regarding whether or not a full performance rating needs to be prepared before you inform an employee of unacceptable performance. Remember, regardless of whatever agency requirements apply, no employee likes to feel "sandbagged" at appraisal time, so confront the poor performance as soon as you become aware of it.

Question: Should my employee get a copy of all my notes about his or her performance?

Answer: As a general rule, you should give your employee a copy of the notes from a discussion or meeting that pertain to your expectations and responsibilities as well as the employee's responsibilities. It is expected that you may take "supervisory" notes to serve as "memory joggers" regarding the employee's performance. For example, these notes can include dates or the number of times an employee was given an instruction. This type of "supervisory" information does not have to be included in the notes given to the employee. Contact your agency's legal counsel or human resources staff for information on Privacy Act requirements concerning supervisory notes.

STEP

1

Question: I've never had to counsel an employee before. What kind of information is worth putting into "supervisory" notes?

Answer: One of the most important things to remember in taking notes is to date them so they reflect when you met with an employee or when you noted a particularly good or bad instance of performance. Keep track of specific examples of poor performance on work assignments. Doing so will make it easier for you to explain what's wrong with the employee's performance through the use of examples. Note how you expressed your performance expectations and how the employee responded to the counseling. Once an opportunity period (see Step Two for an explanation of an opportunity period) has begun, you will need to make notes of all routine meetings with the employee. In addition, you may need to keep a record of when assignments were given to the employee and what instructions were provided.

Question: This person is the first employee with "unacceptable performance" I've ever had in our group. When I looked at the performance standards, I found out that he isn't even doing the work described in them. What now?

Answer: Your first step always should be to convey a clear message to the employee about what your performance expectations are. Performance standards that do not relate to the job need to be rewritten so there will be no confusion between your oral instructions or written guidance and the performance standards themselves. If the new standards that you have written are substantially different from the old ones, you will need to give the employee a chance to work under the new standards before you determine whether or not the employee's performance is unacceptable. As discussed later in Step Three, you do not always need to rely on formal performance standards, depending on the legal authority under which you take action. But you run a serious risk of either having your action overturned or mitigated upon appeal if the employee can demonstrate that his or her performance expectations were not clear.

Counseling Employees About Performance Problems

Additional guidance is presented below on preparing for and conducting counseling sessions.

PREPARING FOR A COUNSELING SESSION

---

1 Once you recognize that a performance problem exists, find out about what guidance the employee has been given on performance. Nine times out of ten, that guidance exists only in performance standards that were issued early. But you may also have some applicable operating manuals or guides, so take a look at everything.

2 Read the performance standards. If they don't really describe what you want from the employee, take the time to fix them. If your organization uses generic standards that cannot be modified, think through the types of things that you will say to the employee to further explain what it is you expect. Write these notes down.

3 Even though you may never need to go any further than an oral counseling session to get this employee to improve, take the time to contact the human resources office and find out what your technical advisor would say if you do need to take formal action later. Ask that specialist to review the performance standards to ensure that there aren't any problems with them.

4 If you do have operating manuals, guides, or other tools that all employees use, take a look at them and see how these could be used to help the employee improve. Try to read them as objectively as possible to look for areas that may not be clear. Remember, you know this job (probably better than almost everybody else), but there is some part of the job that is not making sense or becoming clear to this employee. If you have to, break it down into parts and explain it from the bottom up.

5 Remember your goal is to improve the employee's performance, not to win an argument with the employee. To prepare for a counseling session with an employee, write out and then practice saying what acceptable performance in the job would mean. Listen to yourself. If it doesn't make any sense to you, it won't make any sense to the employee. Be as specific as possible.

6 Have some specific examples of poor performance in your mind (or your notes) so that you can respond to the inevitable, "What do you mean?" Do not emphasize past poor performance, though; instead, seek to clarify future good performance.

CONDUCTING THE COUNSELING SESSION

1 In scheduling a meeting to discuss a performance issue, make sure you allow adequate time for your comments and any feedback from the employee. Whenever possible, conduct the meeting in a private place where the employee will not be embarrassed if the conversation is overheard by coworkers.

2 Choose your time based on your knowledge of the employee. Is this someone who needs to have a meeting like this on Friday so he or she can sort things out over the weekend? Or is this a person who will feel like you are dumping on him or her and then leaving no opportunity to respond for 2 days? Use the same thought process for deciding how information is best given. Although you will be meeting to have a discussion, would this employee like to read through some written notes before talking? Would a verbal discussion with a commitment to follow up with something in writing be more in the style of the employee?

3 Set and maintain a constructive tone: be calm, professional, and focused.

4 Seek cooperation, not confrontation, by focusing on how the employee's performance fits into the performance of the total organization.

5 Unless you think the employee will attempt to take control of the discussion, choose several points throughout your comments where you can stop and get confirmation from the employee that he or she understands the problems and your expectations. Providing opportunities for him or her to respond will allow the employee to be active in the discussion and may lessen the negative connotation of a "lecture" from the boss.

6 At the conclusion of the meeting, end on a positive note by emphasizing that improving the employee's performance is a mutually beneficial goal. Offer a written summary then or to be given to the employee later. Having a written summary is particularly valuable if you will be trying something new or changing any work assignment routine.

7 Keep notes for yourself documenting the date of the discussion and any specific agreements you reached with the employee regarding changes to the way work is assigned or structured.

8 Follow up! If the employee shows improvement, let him or her know it immediately! If the employee appears to be still struggling, go back and talk again.

STEP
2

PROVIDING AN OPPORTUNITY TO IMPROVE

STEP TWO: PROVIDING AN OPPORTUNITY TO IMPROVE

Providing an Opportunity To Improve

Before you even begin the formal process of taking a performance-based action, please be aware that you have certain options. The law provides for two different processes for taking performance-based actions. If a performance-based action is taken under Title 5 CFR Part 432, a formal opportunity to improve is required. If a performance-based action is taken under Title 5 CFR Part 752, an opportunity period is not required. Step Two will walk you through the Part 432 process of giving an employee a formal opportunity to improve his or her performance. (Step Three will provide more details on deciding under which process to take your action.) Regardless of the process you use, an opportunity period is a useful tool for assisting employees in improving their performance.

The Opportunity Period

In most cases, the informal steps you take with employees, such as the counseling described previously in Step One, will prove very effective in your efforts to avoid or resolve poor performance. However, if an employee is still working at an unacceptable level in one or more critical elements, you will need to give the employee a formal opportunity to improve his or her performance.

> Over the years, agencies have developed different mechanisms for providing employees with a formal opportunity to improve unacceptable performance. Many agencies have adopted the use of the Performance Improvement Plan, often referred to as a "PIP." In this booklet, we will use the term "opportunity period" as a generic reference to a formal period for improving unacceptable performance.

This period is designed to give the employee an opportunity to bring his or her performance up to an acceptable level. It is also the supervisor's opportunity to clearly express his or her expectations and the consequences of not meeting those expectations. If the employee fails to improve to an acceptable level by the end of the opportunity period, further action is warranted.

> Under the current regulations for performance appraisal (5 CFR Part 430), there are three types of performance elements: critical, non-critical, and additional. But remember, you can only remove or demote an employee for unacceptable performance in a critical element.

Depending on the nature of the job and the employee's experience, it may be appropriate to offer assistance in a variety of ways. For example, an employee may be given a checklist, paired with another employee, offered training, and/or given closer supervision. Not every employee will require every type of assistance, but once assistance is offered, be sure to follow through with it in the opportunity period. The procedures for providing a formal opportunity to improve are:

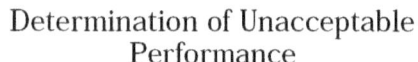

Determination of Unacceptable Performance

Employee's performance is determined to be unacceptable in one or more critical elements.

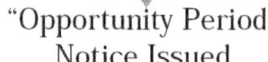

"Opportunity Period" Notice Issued

Inform the employee in writing of the critical element(s) in which he or she is failing, what is needed to bring performance up to an acceptable level, what assistance will be provided, and the consequences of failing to improve during the opportunity period. (See sample notice in the Appendix.)

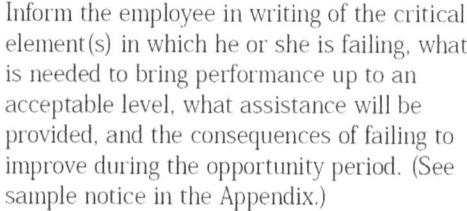

Formal Opportunity To Improve

Employee must bring performance up to an acceptable level in failed critical element(s). Duration of opportunity period may vary. Be sure to document the employee's progress and to provide any appropriate assistance.

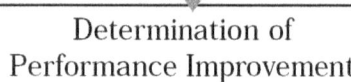

Determination of Performance Improvement

Consider the evidence of performance and compare with standards and expectations outlined in the opportunity period notice.

Hopefully, an employee will improve and maintain acceptable performance. However, if an employee fails to perform acceptably by the end of the opportunity period or improves but then fails again in the same critical element within 1 year from the start of the opportunity period, the supervisor may demote or remove the employee without going through another opportunity period.

Special Considerations

In reality, performance-based actions do not always run as smoothly as the procedures just described. Some issues may occur that deserve special consideration.

Requests for Accommodations

When counseling, providing an opportunity period, or taking action, you may discover that a performance problem is due to a mental or physical condition. As a result, an employee may request some type of accommodation. If the accommodation request does not cause the agency an undue hardship, you are required to accommodate the employee if he or she has a disability and is a "qualified" individual with a disability. This type of situation is an area in which you will have to get technical assistance from your agency's human resources staff. However, as a starting point in your determination as to whether or not an employee is entitled to such an accommodation, review the checklist below.

Does the employee have a disability?

Yes if . . .

✓ Medical documentation supports a physical or mental condition that substantially limits one or more major life activities, or

✓ A record of impairment exists that substantially limits one or more major life activities.

Is the employee a "qualified disabled" person?

Yes if . . .

✓ The employee can perform essential functions with or without reasonable accommodation.

✓ There is no endangerment of health and safety of employee or coworkers.

✓ The employee otherwise meets the requirements of the position.

If the employee demonstrates that he or she is a qualified individual with a disability, you will need to work with your human resources office to determine whether the accommodation request will cause an undue hardship.

Does the accommodation request cause an undue hardship?

Consider the following factors . . .

✓ The number of employees in the organization.

✓ The type of facilities.

✓ The size of the organization's budget.

✓ The cost of the requested accommodation(s).

An accommodation should be designed to address an employee's physical or mental limitations so that the employee has as much of a chance to achieve acceptable performance as a non-disabled person. While each case may be different, as a supervisor your responsibility is to resolve the performance problem, not the mental or physical disability. Keep in mind that a request for accommodation does not preclude you from proceeding with a performance-based action. In many situations, accommodations can be put be in place at the same time an opportunity period is started.

Requests for Leave

Another issue that sometimes "stumps" supervisors is what to do when an employee requests leave during the opportunity period. You should consider each request for leave based on the specific circumstances in the request. Know your agency's rules for approving or disapproving leave and get some technical advice from the human resources office before you deny any leave during this time. Additionally, keep these thoughts in mind:

- An employee on approved leave (annual, sick, or leave without pay) cannot be penalized for work that is not completed while on approved leave.

- An employee should be aware of agency (or office) procedures for requesting leave and for providing medical documentation (especially important for accommodation requests). The employee should also be aware of what action the agency may take if these procedures are not followed.

- Be sure you understand the various family-friendly leave entitlements available to employees, such as the *Family and Medical Leave Act of 1993* and the *Family Friendly Leave Act of 1994.*

- If an employee is on approved leave for a significant period of time during the opportunity period, you may want to extend the period to allow the employee a "reasonable" time on the job to improve.

Deciding What Comes Next

Deciding what comes next depends on the employee's performance at the conclusion of the opportunity period. If the employee has reached an acceptable level of performance, there is no need for any action except to keep providing feedback and encouragement to the employee. If the employee is still performing unacceptably, you must determine the best solution. Your options include reassignment, demotion, or removal (see the flowchart below). Although Governmentwide regulations allow supervisors to choose any of these options, your agency may have some internal rules about considering reassignment before the other choices. Before you reach a decision on what to do, find out from your human resources staff what your responsibilities are.

No Improvement During Opportunity Period

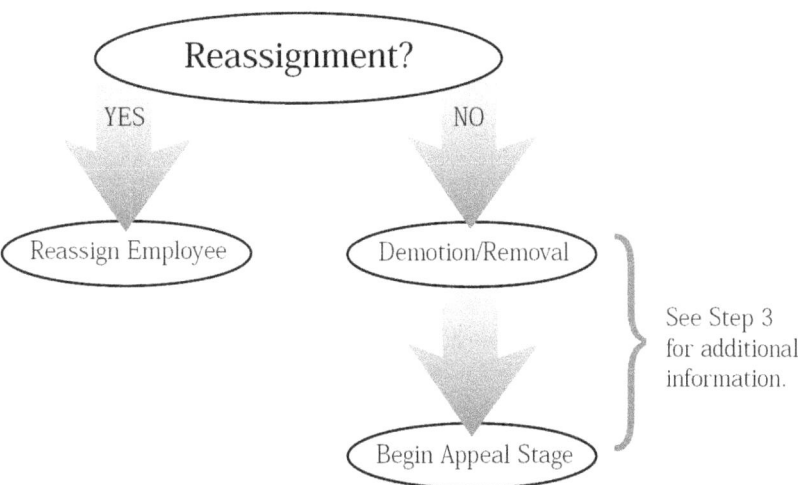

Supervisors may reassign employees without conducting the formal process outlined in the next step. Step Three explains the procedures used after you have decided to demote or remove an employee. This next section also explains the employee's appeal rights.

STEP
2

Use the following checklist to make sure that you have completed all the actions related to Step Two.

Step Two Checklist	Yes	No
In the opportunity notice did you tell the employee that his or her work was unacceptable in one or more critical elements?	❑	❑
Did the opportunity notice tell the employee specifically what he or she had to do to improve performance in order to keep his or her job?	❑	❑
Did you explain what efforts would be made to assist the employee (including training, if appropriate)?	❑	❑
Was the notice clear that continuing failure to meet performance standards would result in demotion or removal?	❑	❑
Did you provide the promised assistance (training, etc.) to the employee?	❑	❑
Did you consider any requests for accommodation?	❑	❑
Did you document the employee's performance during this opportunity period?	❑	❑
Did you take into account any approved annual, sick, or other leave during the opportunity period?	❑	❑
When the opportunity period ended, was the employee still performing at an unacceptable level?	❑	❑
If the employee succeeds in raising his or her performance to an acceptable level, remind the employee of his or her continuing obligation to maintain acceptable performance.		

Step Two Questions and Answers

Question: Is there a law that requires me to allow an employee to bring a union representative into a meeting where I plan to issue an opportunity period notice?

Answer: Because the meeting is not disciplinary or investigatory in nature, you are not obligated to allow union representation. The purpose of the meeting is to explain your expectations of the employee and describe any specific efforts you will be making to assist the employee in improving his or her performance. Although any employee who is being told that his or her work is unacceptable will view this as a negative process, it is a meeting to discuss methods of assisting an employee and is not disciplinary or punitive in nature.

Question: How will I know if my employee is "disabled" and should be accommodated?

Answer: The question of who is "disabled" under the law is one that is still confusing to experts. In most cases, you will want to turn over any documentation you receive from the employee to the human resources office so that they can obtain a physician's review of the employee's medical documentation. Once you get a decision from the medical experts that the employee's condition significantly impacts his or her ability to perform, you will need to carefully consider what the employee is requesting in the way of accommodation and assess whether or not you can provide the accommodation.

Question: What should I do about an employee who just won't talk to me? How can I give this person an opportunity to improve?

Answer: Although we focus a great deal in this booklet on supervisory responsibilities for informing and assisting an employee, the employee has the primary responsibility for improving his or her performance. An employee who gives the boss "the silent treatment" and refuses to accept any assistance runs the risk of failing to improve performance during the opportunity period and suffering the consequences. You may want to consider contacting your human resources office and asking if the agency uses trained mediators or facilitators to break through some communication problems. Regardless, an employee needs to be told what the expectations are for his or her performance and the consequences if these expectations are not met. Be sure to document your efforts to communicate these expectations and consequences.

Question: If my employee asks for leave during the opportunity period, do I have to grant it?

Answer: Generally, annual leave and leave without pay are discretionary based on the needs of the office and could be denied based on the importance of focusing on improving performance in the time allotted. However, sick leave, supported by acceptable documentation, must be approved as long as the employee follows agency procedures for requesting the leave. As noted earlier, you should be aware of certain programs under the Family and Medical Leave Act of 1993 and the Family Friendly Leave Act of 1994 that may require you to approve leave.

Question: If I do approve leave during an opportunity period, what happens to the deadlines that I've set up?

Answer: Once you approve leave, you cannot hold the employee accountable for work that does not get done during the absence. In terms of short absences, you may not have to adjust the deadlines or requirements at all. However, if the employee is out for an extended time during the opportunity period, you may need to extend the opportunity period for the time of the absence to ensure that the employee has a chance to perform acceptably. Depending upon the nature of the work, an opportunity period shortened by approved absence may be valid if the work assignments and expectations were such that the employee still had the chance to demonstrate improved performance.

Question: We don't have any money for training. What should I do about training during the opportunity period?

Answer: There is no requirement for formal classroom training. One option is to see how much of the training can be accomplished with the experts on your own staff. On-the-job training is probably the most common form of training provided during an opportunity period. Also, contact your agency training officer and find out what is available through self-instructional manuals, videos, or agency-funded training programs.

Question: Do I have to follow the counseling steps before initiating an opportunity period?

Answer: There is no legal obligation to provide counseling to an employee before beginning an opportunity period because of the employee's unacceptable performance. However, it is always good management practice to talk to an employee when his or her performance begins to slip below the acceptable level. Hopefully, early counseling efforts would be successful and there would be no need for a formal opportunity period.

STEP
3

TAKING
ACTION

STEP THREE: TAKING ACTION

Taking Action

This section is designed to give you an overview of the process used in taking action for unacceptable performance. It will describe the role and responsibilities of the proposing official and deciding official. There is also a brief explanation of employee appeal rights.

A Supervisor's Authority

A supervisor has the authority to take action against an employee based on poor performance in accordance with Title 5 Code of Federal Regulations Part 432, Performance Based Reduction in Grade and Removal Actions, and Part 752, Adverse Actions. Although it may strike you as peculiar that a performance deficiency would be handled through adverse action procedures, there are times supervisors determine that using Part 752 procedures, which differ from Part 432 requirements, is the most appropriate method of taking action. The specific facts of your case, along with the weight of your evidence, will be determining factors in deciding under which authority to take your action. To help you understand the differences in these regulations, Figures A and B describe the procedures for taking a performance-based action under Parts 432 and 752, respectively. Figure C compares these regulations to further clarify the differences between each authority.

Figure A. Elements of a Part 432 Action

Demotion and Removal Based on Unacceptable Performance Under 5 CFR Part 432	
1. Beginning of appraisal period	Give employee the performance elements and standards in writing. Establish which elements are critical.
2. Informal steps to improve performance	Provide discussion, counseling, training, etc.
3. Formal opportunity to improve	Establish a formal period to show acceptable performance.
4. Notice of proposed action	Give employee 30 days advance written notice; only specify instances of unacceptable performance occurring in the past year and relating to the critical elements involved.
5. Employee's answer to proposal notice	Provide a reasonable time to reply; employee has a right to representation.
6. Decision issued	Issue decision within 30 days after notice period expires; a higher level official concurs with the decision.
7. Notice of right to appeal	Give employee appeal rights information.

Figure B. Elements of a Part 752 Action

Suspension, Demotion, and Removal Based on Unacceptable Performance Under 5 CFR Part 752	
1. Informal steps to improve performance deficiencies	Provide discussion, counseling, training, etc.
2. Notice of proposed action	Give employee 30 days advance written notice.
3. Employee's answer to proposal notice	Provide a reasonable time to reply, not less than 7 days.
4. Decision issued	No requirement exists for higher level review.
5. Notice of right to appeal	Give employee appeal rights information.

STEP
3

Figure C. Comparison of Part 432 vs. Part 752

5 CFR Part 432 vs. Part 752		
	PART 432	PART 752
Types of Actions	Actions: Demotion or Removal	Actions: Suspension, Demotion, or Removal
Actions Taken For	Actions taken for "unacceptable performance."	Actions taken for "such cause as will promote the efficiency of the service."
Proof	Actions must be proven by "substantial evidence" (lower standard than Part 752).	Actions must be proven by a "preponderance of the evidence" (higher standard than Part 432).
Actions Based On	Actions can only be based on an employee's formal, established, communicated standards.	Actions can be based on expectations or established/formal standards.
Opportunity Period	Employee is entitled to an opportunity period.	No requirement for an opportunity period.
Time Limits	Time limited to performance "deficiencies" occurring within the 1 year prior to the proposal notice.	No time limit for inclusion of "incident/charges" in Part 752.
Immediacy of Action	Employee remains on the job throughout the opportunity period.	Can take immediate action because no requirement for an opportunity period exists.
Mitigation	Action may not be mitigated (action will either be sustained or reversed).	Action may be mitigated (penalty reduced).

As you can see, there are distinct differences between these regulations. For example, Part 432 requires that you give the employee an opportunity to bring his or her performance up to an acceptable level, while Part 752 does not require such an opportunity period. With this difference in mind, you may question the reasoning behind providing an opportunity period if it is not required. Keep in mind that third parties (for example, arbitrators, judges) place a strong emphasis on a supervisor's effort to communicate what is expected to the employee as well as the supervisor's effort to assist the employee in improving his or her performance. An opportunity period addresses both of these concerns. While an opportunity period may not be required under Part 752, providing such an opportunity may assist the agency in developing a stronger case before a third party.

Another difference between the regulations is that Part 432 requires the use of established performance elements and standards. Under Part 752, employees can be held to ad hoc standards such as explicit instructions or work assignments or professional standards established for certain occupations such as physicians. In some cases, it may be more appropriate to hold employees to these ad hoc standards, as long as they are no more stringent than the established performance standards. As always, consult with your human resources staff to determine if the use of ad hoc standards or if a formal opportunity period is appropriate in your specific case. Also, talk with your human resources staff concerning any internal agency policies regarding the use of a formal opportunity period.

Appeal Rights

Employees will generally have the right to appeal a removal or demotion to the Merit Systems Protection Board or to grieve the action through the agency's negotiated grievance procedure. The employee can choose between these two methods of appeal, but cannot pursue both avenues. Allegations of discrimination, reprisal for whistleblowing, and other prohibited personnel practices can be raised in an employee's appeal. Such allegations can also be filed directly with your agency's Equal Employment Office or the Office of Special Counsel.

Regardless of the route an employee chooses to appeal a performance-based action, following the guidance in this booklet and getting assistance as needed from your agency's human resources staff and legal counsel will prepare you to present a strong case supporting your actions before any third party. Remember—the staffs of those two offices are the experts in this area, and will be glad to explain your role in the appeals process and provide the technical assistance you need.

Use the following checklist to make sure that you have completed all the actions related to Step Three.

Step Three Checklist	Yes	No
For Actions Based on 5 CFR Part 432		
Do you have written performance standards/elements for the employee?	❏	❏
Do you have copies of any supervisory notes of counseling or assistance given to the employee?	❏	❏
Do you have copies of memoranda of counseling provided to the employee?	❏	❏
Do you have a copy of the written notice providing an opportunity to improve?	❏	❏
Did you document the employee's performance during the opportunity period?	❏	❏

For Actions Based on 5 CFR Part 752	Yes	No
Do you have written performance standards/elements for the employee OR evidence that performance expectations were communicated?	❏	❏
Is there documentation that the employee was clearly "on notice" of performance expectations?	❏	❏
Do you have copies of any supervisory notes of counseling or assistance given to the employee?	❏	❏
Do you have copies of memoranda of counseling provided to the employee?	❏	❏
Do you have a copy of the written notice providing an opportunity to improve OR can you explain your reasons for not providing an opportunity to improve?	❏	❏
Did you document the employee's performance during the period in question?	❏	❏

Step Three Questions and Answers

Question: How much specific information needs to go into a proposal notice to remove?

Answer: We have provided a sample of an action proposed under Part 432 in the appendix to this booklet, but the real answer to this question lies in your agency. Each agency has a "culture" that defines the amount of information and documentation that will go into a proposal notice. At a minimum, your notice will state which regulation the action is being taken under, specify what critical performance element(s) the employee failed to meet, cite the evidence of unacceptable performance, and discuss the opportunity period (or the lack of one). The notice will also explain to the employee the time allowed for a written and/or oral response. Ask your human resources specialist for some samples of other performance-based notices to get a sense of what your agency requires.

Question: What reasons warrant not providing an employee with a formal opportunity period to improve?

Answer: As stated earlier, if you take a performance-based action under Part 432, you must provide an employee with a formal opportunity to improve. On the other hand, Part 752 does not require a supervisor to provide an employee with such an opportunity. One reason for not providing an opportunity period may be that your employee has several years of experience in the job and additional training would prove useless. Another reason may be that your employee has already received extensive informal training and additional training or assistance would seem unreasonable.

Question: What if I fail to issue my Part 432 decision within 30 days after the notice period expires?

Answer: The regulations require that an employee receive a decision in Part 432 actions within 30 days of the expiration of the 30-day notice period. This provision automatically gives you a 60-day period of time in which to work. Additionally, the Office of Personnel Management has issued regulations that give agencies the discretion to extend the initial 30-day notice period by another 30 days, so you are actually working within a 90-day timeframe. However, there are always those situations where even more time will be needed, perhaps because the employee has asked for a lengthy extension to prepare a response or the deciding official cannot gather and analyze all the information needed within the 90 days allowed. 5 CFR Part 432 lists six reasons that commonly cause delay and allows agencies to extend the notice period if those conditions exist. If your situation does not fall into any of the six categories, the regulations provide that OPM can approve an extension of the notice period based on a brief written request by the agency.

Question: How should I decide whether to suspend, demote, or remove?

Answer: This answer depends largely on whether you proceed under Part 432 or Part 752. Under Part 432, you have the option of demotion or removal and you do not have to defend your reasoning for choosing either action. As was noted in Figure C, mitigation to a lesser action by a third party is not possible. So, if you meet the requirements of proving that the employee was unacceptable, even after being given an opportunity to improve, no third party can challenge your reasons for removing instead of demoting the employee. Therefore, your decision is based on your analysis of whether the employee can function acceptably in a lower graded position or not. Some agencies may have policies that require supervisors to explore demotion options before going to removal, but that policy would be an internal policy, not one that governs all Federal supervisors.

However, reduction in the agency-selected penalty, known as mitigation, is a possibility in any action taken under Part 752. Therefore, you will need to explain in any decision notice, and possibly in a proposal notice as well, what factors led you to believe that your chosen action (suspension, demotion, or removal) was the right one. Most supervisors who have taken any kind of adverse action against an employee have been told about the Douglas factors. This is a reference to a decision by the Merit Systems Protection Board that listed 12 factors that might be taken into consideration when deciding on the appropriate penalty in any adverse action. Your human resources office will be able to provide you with a copy of these factors. At this point, it is sufficient to understand that the factors force a deciding official to examine any issues that might support a more severe penalty as well as those circumstances that would convince the deciding official to lower the penalty.

STEP
3

SPECIAL
TOPICS

SPECIAL TOPICS

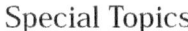

Special Topics

During the process of addressing and resolving performance problems, you will need to keep abreast of certain situations that are driven by an employee's length of service. The two most common situations involve the consideration of an employee's probationary/trial period and the denial of his or her within-grade increase.

The Probationary/Trial Period

One of the most important times to address performance is during the probationary/trial period. As the final step in the examination process of a new employee, this period—which generally lasts 1 to 2 years—is designed to give supervisors the opportunity to assess how well an employee can perform the duties of a job.

> PROBATIONARY PERIOD (1 YEAR) = COMPETITIVE SERVICE EMPLOYEES
>
> TRIAL PERIOD (1 TO 2 YEARS) = EXCEPTED SERVICE EMPLOYEES

Employees' performance during this time period usually serves as a good indication of how well they will perform throughout their career. During this period, supervisors should provide assistance to help new employees improve their performance while, at the same time, determine whether or not the employee is suited for a position.

If a performance-based action is warranted against a probationer, please keep in mind that probationers can appeal their termination to the Merit Systems Protection Board only if their termination is based on marital status or partisan political affiliation. Employees working during their probationary/trial periods are not covered under Parts 432 or 752 of the Code of Federal Regulations. This exemption is due, in part, to the fact that the very nature of this period is to allow supervisors the chance to determine whether a new employee will be an asset rather than a liability to the organization.

> The lapse of a probationary/trial period without a proper assessment of a new employee's performance may result in future performance problems. For supervisors, the probationary/trial period should always be considered a key period for addressing and resolving poor performance.

SPECIAL TOPICS

Within-Grade Increase Denials

While in the process of assisting an employee with improving performance, or sometimes in the process of taking a performance-based action, a supervisor often has to deal with the issue of a within-grade increase denial. Within-grade increases (often called WIGI) are routinely granted for employees whose performance is acceptable, but supervisors need to be aware of the process required to "deny" a within-grade increase when an employee's performance is not at the acceptable level.

In order to be eligible for a within-grade increase, an employee must be performing at an "acceptable level of competence." In most agencies, this eligibility requires a rating of fully successful or equivalent. Depending on the nature of an agency's performance management system, it is not unusual for an employee to be above the unacceptable level but below the level required for a within-grade increase.

As soon as you determine that an employee's performance is falling below the acceptable level, even if it is not yet at the unacceptable level, find out when the employee's next within-grade increase is due. Depending upon the step of the employee, there may be a 1-, 2-, or 3-year waiting period until the next within-grade increase could be granted. If it is coming up anytime soon, you need to assess where the employee stands in terms of meeting the standards for an overall rating of acceptable performance.

Special Topics: Key Points To Remember

Following are key points to remember about the special topics presented in this section.

Probationary Employees

✓ A probationary employee can appeal his or her termination for unsatisfactory performance or misconduct to the Merit Systems Protection Board only if he or she can allege discrimination due to marital status or political partisan affiliation.

✓ A probationary/trial period, depending on the type of appointment, generally lasts only 1 to 2 years. In your efforts to avoid future performance problems, be sure to make a thorough assessment of a new employee's performance during this period.

Within-Grade Increases

✓ Granting of within-grade increases is determined based on meeting the appropriate waiting period and having the most recent rating of record be at an acceptable level of competence or better.

✓ To grant a within-grade increase, you must issue a determination that the employee is demonstrating an "acceptable level of competence" as documented in a current rating (i.e., not more than 1 year old).

✓ Once a within-grade increase has been denied, a supervisor has the flexibility to approve a within-grade increase at any time thereafter once the employee is determined to be performing at an acceptable level of competence, but the agency must consider the employee's performance at least every 52 weeks after the denial.

SPECIAL TOPICS

 Special Topics: Questions and Answers

Question: Do I have to give a probationary/trial employee an opportunity to improve?

Answer: No. The law and regulations specifically exclude probationary/trial employees from the procedures that require the use of an opportunity to improve. This exclusion is because the entire probationary period is similar to an opportunity period. These employees should receive closer supervision, instruction, and training as needed during the first year of their employment.

Question: What happens when a within-grade increase comes due right in the middle of an opportunity period?

Answer: Technically, the within-grade increase determination is based on the most recent rating of record as long as it was issued within the last year. However, the regulations provide that a supervisor, in making an "acceptable level of competence" determination, may issue a new rating if the most recent rating does not reflect the employee's current performance.

Consider the case where an employee's within-grade increase is due in 3 weeks, the last rating was Fully Successful, and the employee was given an opportunity to improve that began last month. You would need to decide whether the employee's current performance has come back up to Fully Successful, and if so, you would approve the within-grade increase. However, it is more likely that the current performance is still below the acceptable level, in which case a new rating needs to be issued to support the denial of the within-grade increase.

SPECIAL TOPICS

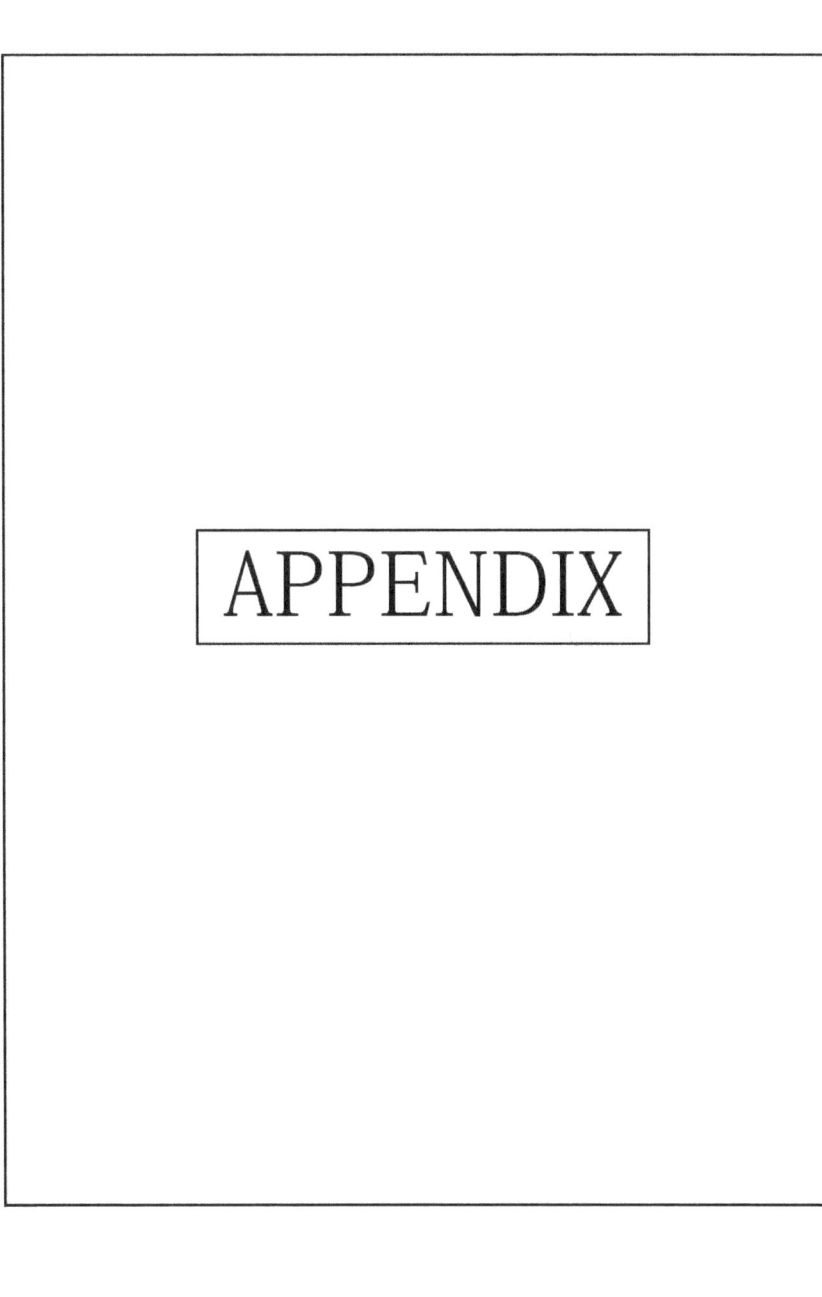

APPENDIX

APPENDIX

APPENDIX

Contents

This appendix contains samples of documentation provided by a supervisor to an employee at different stages in the process of addressing performance problems.

Specific items contained in this appendix include the following:

- Sample Memorandum of Counseling

- Sample Opportunity Notice: Example #1

- Sample Opportunity Notice: Example #2

- Sample Proposal Notice

- Sample Decision Notice

SAMPLE MEMORANDUM OF COUNSELING

SUBJECT   MEMORANDUM OF COUNSELING

FROM   DANA SMITH, ASSISTANT DIRECTOR
                 OFFICE OF INFORMATION TECHNOLOGY

TO   PAMELA WASHINGTON
                 COMPUTER SPECIALIST

The purpose of this memo is to provide a summary of our August 20th meeting. This meeting was held to informally discuss your performance during the implementation of a new local area network (LAN). As I said last Tuesday, there are three areas of concern with your work. My ...

SAMPLE OPPORTUNITY NOTICE: EXAMPLE #1

SUBJECT   NOTIFICATION OF UNACCEPTABLE PERFORMANCE/
                 OPPORTUNITY TO IMPROVE

FROM   TUAN LEUNG
                 CHIEF, ACCOUNTING AND FINANCE DIVISION

TO   ANGIE SMITH
                 ACCOUNTING TECHNICIAN

This notice is written confirmation that I am providing you with an opportunity to improve your performance to the Minimally Successful level. I have determined that your performance is unacceptable in two critical elements of your position, and therefore, a performance improvement plan (PIP) is required under Article 10 of our Collective Bargaining Agreement. The PIP outlines ...

SAMPLE OPPORTUNITY NOTICE: EXAMPLE #2

SUBJECT   NOTIFICATION OF UNACCEPTABLE PERFORMANCE/
                 OPPORTUNITY TO IMPROVE

FROM   MARIA SANCHEZ
                 CHIEF, EMPLOYEE RELATIONS DIVISION

TO   JOHN BROOME
                 EMPLOYEE RELATIONS SPECIALIST

Since your mid-year progress review on January 6th, your performance has declined steadily and has reached the Unacceptable level. You have not improved in any of the areas we discussed during the mid-year review, nor has your performance improved in response to counseling sessions and memoranda that you have received over the past few months. I have determined that you are ...

SAMPLE PROPOSAL NOTICE

SUBJECT   PROPOSAL TO REMOVE FOR
          UNACCEPTABLE PERFORMANCE

FROM   MARIA SANCHEZ, CHIEF
          EMPLOYEE RELATIONS DIVISION

TO   JOHN BROOME
          EMPLOYEE RELATIONS SPECIALIST

This is to inform you that I propose to remove you from your position as Employee Relations Specialist, GS-230-13, and from the Federal Service, for unacceptable performance under the provisions of 5 CFR Part 432. This proposal is based upon your unacceptable performance in the following critical element: Providing Technical Assistance to Managers. This action, if taken, will ...

SAMPLE DECISION NOTICE

SUBJECT   DECISION TO REMOVE FOR
                 UNACCEPTABLE PERFORMANCE

FROM   BEN TAYLOR, ASSISTANT DIRECTOR
                 FOR ADMINISTRATION

TO   JOHN BROOME
                 EMPLOYEE RELATIONS SPECIALIST

In a notice dated and received by you on October 20th, Maria Sanchez, Chief of Employee Relations, proposed to remove you from your position of Employee Relations Specialist, GS-230-13, and from the Federal Service, on the basis of unacceptable performance.

As the deciding official, I have carefully reviewed all the material that formed the basis for the proposal and that was also made available for your review. I have also given full consideration to our meeting of November 2nd, during which you presented your oral response to the proposed removal as well as your written response. While you mentioned several times that you believed I had already made up my mind about this case and that your response was meaningless, you nevertheless challenged, in general terms, the validity of the opportunity period and alluded to many technical inaccuracies. Despite my request that you provide me with a listing of specific errors that occurred in the course of the opportunity period, you never did so. Without any specific information, I cannot give your statements any weight in my considerations. Nonetheless, I have reviewed the documentation for technical inaccuracies and have found none.

You did state that you believed you had a heavier workload than the other specialists in the branch and that it was not possible to keep up with all of the calls from supervisors who needed assistance. However, I have reviewed the monthly case report from your branch and have found that you were assigned approximately the same number of cases to handle as your colleagues during June and July and were given fewer cases, comparatively, during the month of August. Secondly, your cases were not the most complex or arduous available. Although several were complicated, I found nothing of a difficulty that a specialist at the grade 13 level should not be expected to handle.

I cannot, therefore, find any justification for your continuing failure to contact supervisors in a timely manner or your failure to meet your assigned deadlines. The evidence in the proposal notice and evidence file clearly indicates that you failed to meet the requirements for Fully Successful performance regarding the timeliness of your work.

You did not specifically respond to the issue of your failure to provide accurate technical guidance to supervisors and managers. I find the evidence compelling that your supervisor attempted to give you a mechanism for reviewing current case law and ensuring that your advice reflected any ...

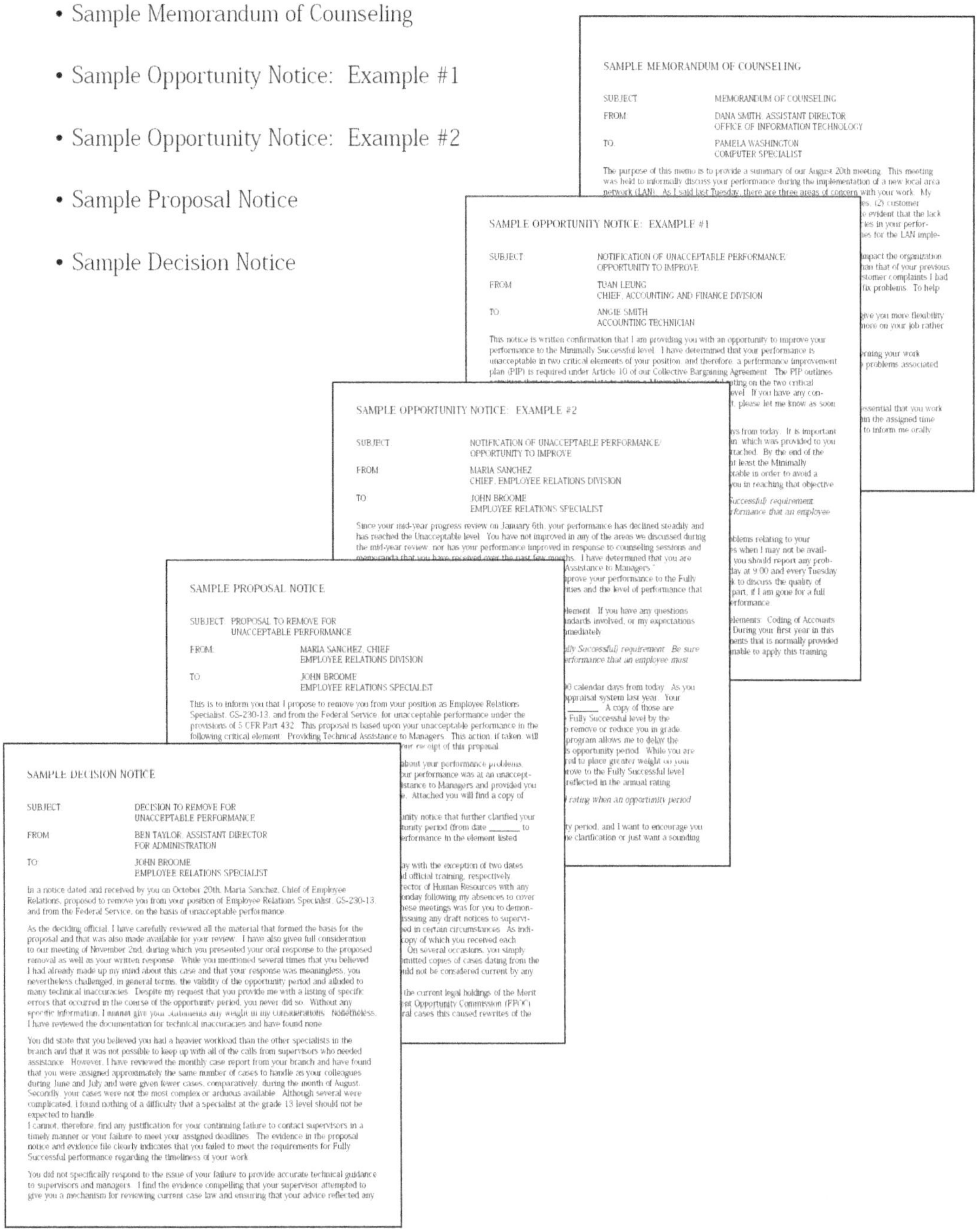

APPENDIX

APPENDIX

SAMPLE MEMORANDUM OF COUNSELING

SUBJECT: MEMORANDUM OF COUNSELING

FROM: DANA SMITH, ASSISTANT DIRECTOR
OFFICE OF INFORMATION TECHNOLOGY

TO: PAMELA WASHINGTON
COMPUTER SPECIALIST

The purpose of this memo is to provide a summary of our August 20th meeting. This meeting was held to informally discuss your performance during the implementation of a new local area network (LAN). As I said last Tuesday, there are three areas of concern with your work. My understanding of the issues addressed are as follows: (1) Missed deadlines, (2) customer complaints, and (3) careless mistakes. During our discussion, it was quite evident that the lack of good communication between the two of us has contributed to deficiencies in your performance. Particularly, you noted that although I gave you overall time frames for the LAN implementation, I never explained the importance of specific deadlines and how that would impact the organization. You also said that my style of supervision was more detailed and closer than that of your previous supervisor. Finally, you seemed genuinely surprised by the number of customer complaints I had received about your work and the number of times I had to follow up and fix problems. To help improve your performance, we agreed on the following:

1. While I may not change my "hands-on" management style, I agreed to give you more flexibility to work independently. In turn, this will allow you to be able to focus more on your job rather than worry about what my intentions are.

2. I agreed to inform you of all complaints I receive from customers concerning your work. In turn, you agreed to handle these complaints yourself and correct the problems associated with them.

3. We both agreed to meeting weekly to discuss our progress.

Based on your experience, I believe you can succeed in this job, but it is essential that you work to reduce the number of errors and focus clearly on completing work within the assigned time frames. If you have any comments to add to these notes, please feel free to inform me orally or in writing.

APPENDIX

SAMPLE OPPORTUNITY NOTICE: EXAMPLE #1

SUBJECT: NOTIFICATION OF UNACCEPTABLE PERFORMANCE/
              OPPORTUNITY TO IMPROVE

FROM: TUAN LEUNG
         CHIEF, ACCOUNTING AND FINANCE DIVISION

TO: ANGIE SMITH
      ACCOUNTING TECHNICIAN

This notice is written confirmation that I am providing you with an opportunity to improve your performance to the Minimally Successful level. I have determined that your performance is unacceptable in two critical elements of your position, and therefore, a performance improvement plan (PIP) is required under Article 10 of our Collective Bargaining Agreement. The PIP outlines activities that you must complete to attain a Minimally Successful rating on the two critical elements in which your performance has fallen to an unacceptable level. If you have any concerns about the PIP or you require additional guidance in following it, please let me know as soon as questions arise.

The PIP becomes effective today and will continue for 60 calendar days from today. It is important to perform well under the standards set out in your performance plan, which was provided to you on _____. A copy of the elements and standards for your job is attached. By the end of the opportunity period, you must have brought your performance up to at least the Minimally Successful level on the elements in which you are currently unacceptable in order to avoid a reduction in grade, removal, or reassignment. This PIP is to assist you in reaching that objective.

[This sample uses a performance system with a level 2 (Minimally Successful) requirement. Be sure to review your agency's system to determine the level of performance that an employee must reach to stay in the job.]

During the period of the PIP, you are to report directly to me for problems relating to your performance. Given the nature of my duties, I realize there are times when I may not be available for several hours at a time during the day. During these times, you should report any problems or address your questions to Ron Santilli. Beginning this Tuesday at 9:00 and every Tuesday morning throughout the PIP, you and I will meet at least once a week to discuss the quality of your work. Although I don't foresee any long-term absences on my part, if I am gone for a full week, Ron will act on my behalf and meet with you to review your performance.

The deficiencies in your performance have centered on two critical elements: Coding of Accounts Payable Documents and Performance of Scheduled Reconciliations. During your first year in this job, you received all of the formal training associated with these elements that is normally provided to accounting technicians in this branch. However, you have been unable to apply this training

APPENDIX

and demonstrate the necessary skills in these elements. Your most recent annual performance rating of Fully Successful was given despite the fact that these performance discrepancies existed to some degree even during your first year. I made that decision on the basis that some of those performance problems reflected the fact that you were still in the learning curve on your assignments. These problems were communicated to you during the annual performance review. However, in the 6 months since that rating was given, your work performance has declined and, despite the fact that I have routinely pointed out your errors, you have not been able to perform acceptably in some of the key areas of your position.

In the critical element of "Performance of Scheduled Reconciliations" your performance plan states that the Minimally Successful level of performance is:

Routinely reconciles accounting transactions affecting the employee's assigned work, including obligations, accruals, and payments, in an accurate manner. These transactions are reconciled accurately to the accounts payable open document listing in a timely manner.

Currently, your performance on this critical element is at an unacceptable level due to the number of errors I have found in your work because you continually post transactions in the wrong category and then extensive work is needed to determine why your records are not reconciled. Over the past month, I frequently had to point out to you mistakes that occurred because accounting documents were not input in the appropriate categories in the system. Further, I found that 25 errors occurred where your worksheets did not balance with the open document listing. Although your performance standard does not include numerical requirements, 25 errors in one month does not meet the requirement for routinely accurate work. This type of performance is representative of the performance deficiencies you have been exhibiting over the past several months.

[At this point an actual notice would include a more detailed assessment of the mistakes in the employee's work.]

During this opportunity period, you must improve your performance to at least the Minimally Successful level in order to continue in your position. In particular, you must conduct your reconciliation work with an error rate of no more than 10% per week, in accordance with the requirement for accuracy listed in your standard. You must also reconcile your worksheets with the accounts payable open document listing with an error rate of no more than 10% per week. Each of these two functions within this standard are equally important and failure to perform adequately on either one will result in an overall finding of unacceptable on the standard as a whole.

To assist you in this area, I would like to spend some time during our first weekly meeting next Tuesday to review the reconciliation process and go over with you the thought process that is needed when deciding where certain transactions should go in the system. Please bring with you your reference material from the training class and we will adapt the generic checklist provided in that book to include our internal requirements as well. You can then use that amended checklist as a reference point in the future.

APPENDIX

[Specific examples of various forms of assistance should be included here.]

In the critical element, "Coding of Accounts Payable Documents," your performance plan states that the Minimally Successful level of performance is:

Routinely codes appropriate accounting data from original documentation onto the Document History Record (DHR) in an accurate and timely manner. These data include such entries as the schedule number, cross reference, transaction code, document number, management code, money amount, and vendor name/order number.

Your performance in this element is unacceptable based on both your problems with accurate coding and your lack of timeliness. Although some level of error is anticipated given the large number of data items that must be coded by the technicians in the Branch, the constant number of corrections that you must make on your work is not acceptable. With each of my counseling memos to you, I have attached copies of DHR error reports that reflect the repetitive nature of your errors. Further, as reflected in the "overdue corrections" column of these reports, you often take up to 10 working days to make the correction and return the work for input into the automated system. This creates the potential for an even greater negative impact because any reports generated from those data prior to the correction contain the erroneous information and are also incorrect.

[At this point an actual notice would include a more detailed assessment of the mistakes in the employee's work.]

In order to achieve Minimally Successful performance in this critical element, you will need to reduce your number of errors to no more than 20 coding errors on any biweekly error report. I arrived at the figure of 20 errors based on the fact that the number of data items coded in a 2-week period is typically 300. Here, errors will be defined as coding mistakes in situations where you received all the correct information on the original documentation. Errors that resulted because you were given incorrect information or because the data were changed after they were originally coded will not count against your standard. 95% of the time, corrections to the DHR error report will be made within 5 working days of receipt of the report. Both accuracy and time-liness are equally important in the performance of this critical element, and failure to meet the requirements of either will result in an overall finding of unacceptable on the standard as a whole.

To assist you in improving in this aspect of your job, I have asked Ron Santilli to create a "cheat sheet" of commonly used codes for a variety of entries. I have also pulled up your coding sheets for each of the errors shown on the latest DHR error report. During our first weekly meeting, we will go over each of the mistakes and perhaps I can determine a pattern that may show why you are not selecting the correct codes. Also, each week, bring three or four of your current assignments to the meeting and we will go through the coding together.

I believe that if you use these written tools and our weekly meetings to develop and hone your accounting skills, you will be able to bring your performance to an acceptable level. You must meet and maintain the Minimally Successful level of performance on both the critical elements

APPENDIX

listed above for 1 year from the beginning of the opportunity period. Failure to achieve acceptable performance on these critical elements during the opportunity period, or to maintain it during the remainder of the 1 year, may result in removal or reduction in grade without any further opportunity to demonstrate acceptable performance.

If you have any questions about this PIP or require additional guidance on implementing the provisions of it, please let me know as soon as questions arise. Keep in mind that it is important to refer to this plan throughout the PIP period.

[It is essential that you contact your human resources office to determine what additional information should be included in an actual notice. Agency policies and collective bargaining agreements sometimes provide that specific notice or referrals are given to employees.]

If you feel that you have a personal or medical problem that may be impeding your ability to perform your duties at an acceptable level, I suggest that you seek assistance through the Employee Assistance Program (EAP). This is a confidential program, and you may reach a counselor by calling 1-800-555-1212 to schedule an appointment.

Please sign a copy of this memorandum, which serves only to acknowledge your receipt of this notice.

Receipt Acknowledged

_____   _____

       Signature   Date

APPENDIX

SAMPLE OPPORTUNITY NOTICE: EXAMPLE #2

SUBJECT: NOTIFICATION OF UNACCEPTABLE PERFORMANCE/
OPPORTUNITY TO IMPROVE

FROM: MARIA SANCHEZ
CHIEF, EMPLOYEE RELATIONS DIVISION

TO: JOHN BROOME
EMPLOYEE RELATIONS SPECIALIST

Since your mid-year progress review on January 6th, your performance has declined steadily and has reached the Unacceptable level. You have not improved in any of the areas we discussed during the mid-year review, nor has your performance improved in response to counseling sessions and memoranda that you have received over the past few months. I have determined that you are Unacceptable in the critical element, "Providing Technical Assistance to Managers." Consequently, I am providing you with an opportunity to improve your performance to the Fully Successful level, and this notice outlines the required activities and the level of performance that you must attain in order to be considered Fully Successful on this critical element. If you have any questions concerning the contents of this notice, the performance standards involved, or my expectations of you during the opportunity period, please come to me immediately.

[This sample uses a performance system with a level 3 (Fully Successful) requirement. Be sure to review your agency's system to determine the level of performance that an employee must reach to stay in the job.]

The opportunity period begins today and will continue for 90 calendar days from today. As you are aware, the agency adopted a three-level performance appraisal system last year. Your performance elements and standards were given to you on _____. A copy of those are attached. Therefore, it is essential that you improve to the Fully Successful level by the conclusion of the opportunity period, or I will take action to remove or reduce you in grade. Although your annual rating is due in 3 weeks, our agency program allows me to delay the issuance of your summary rating until the conclusion of this opportunity period. While you are currently performing at an Unacceptable level, I am prepared to place greater weight on your performance during the opportunity period, and, if you improve to the Fully Successful level on this critical element, the improved performance will be reflected in the annual rating.

[Check your agency policies on the issue of delaying a final rating when an opportunity period is in effect.]

We will need to work together closely during the opportunity period, and I want to encourage you to discuss your cases with me at any time that you need some clarification or just want a sounding board for your ideas. At a minimum, we will meet once a week to go over your caseload and work

APPENDIX

through any problem issues. This will also be an opportunity for you to ask questions or seek clarification from me. For my part, I will give you an assessment of your performance progress for the week, provide recommendations for improvement, or give specific assignments and deadlines. We will plan to meet on Thursday afternoons from 2:00 - 3:00 p.m., throughout the opportunity period.

The Fully Successful level of performance in the critical element "Providing Technical Assistance to Managers" states, "Provides accurate and timely advice and technical guidance to supervisors on a full range of issues involving discipline, leave, standards of conduct, and procedures for performance-based and adverse actions." The deficiencies in your performance are basically the same problems we have been discussing for some months. You are an experienced employee relations specialist and have done your job well in the past, but your current work products are plagued by incomplete, haphazard preparation and background work. Additionally, your work is not timely and I am routinely receiving complaints from supervisors that you are not returning their calls in a timely manner and draft documents are not delivered as promised.

Specifically, you and I have discussed several times that it is not appropriate for you to rely on your recollection of case law from the Merit Systems Protection Board (MSPB) and the Equal Employment Opportunity Commission (EEOC). Instead, you must research the current case law whenever you are preparing to give a supervisor advice on how to proceed and certainly before drafting a proposed notice of action based on misconduct or performance problems. While numerous examples of this problem are noted in my counseling notes to you, one example is illustrative. You advised a manager that she could send home an employee who was not "ready, willing, and able" to work and the employee would be forced to use his own leave. The case law on this topic is clear that the MSPB has not allowed the use of enforced leave without adverse action procedures, and it has been years since the "ready, willing, and able" standard was dropped by the Board. Your failure to stop and check the status of the cases in this area caused the supervisor to erroneously place an employee on leave, an action that had to be corrected as soon as I heard about it from a union steward. The supervisor was embarrassed when she had to contact the employee about the correction and was furious for being made to look ignorant. Even after I brought this to your attention, you were adamant that the old case law prevailed and only agreed with me after I ordered you to review the case law from the last 4 years. As noted earlier, additional examples of this type of problem are in the counseling memorandum (dated _____), which I have provided to you.

The other key performance deficiency that we have been discussing is your lack of attention to specific deadlines and a general lack of attentiveness to the supervisors who seek your technical expertise and guidance. In all cases where a supervisor has complained to me about your failure to follow up, I have notified you and asked for an explanation before responding to the manager who raised the issue. Dr. Tiberius, a manager in the finance department, was particularly frustrated when you did not return several of his calls (over a 4-day period) and finally called me to get an answer to a relatively simple question about the procedures for invoking leave under FMLA.

APPENDIX

Similarly, I had to respond to calls from Ms. Capulet, another of your customers, who was in her second week of waiting for a proposed suspension notice. When I asked you about the action, you told me it was a routine AWOL action but you just hadn't gotten to it. Looking at everything else you had responsibility for during that 2-week period, I found no justification for the delay and assigned the notice to another specialist who prepared it in 2 days.

[Actual notices will include more details concerning unacceptable performance. Often data cited to support the determination of unacceptable performance are attached to the notice.]

I recognize that you have many competing demands on your time, but it is essential that you keep supervisors apprised of what you are doing and set realistic timeframes for responding to their inquiries or for drafting memos or notices. A GS-13 is required and expected to make independent judgments and appropriately schedule their work for timely completion. In all of our discussions, you have not articulated a good reason for your failure to return a phone call or deliver a promised draft. Your statement that you are doing your best does not seem viable when large numbers of deadlines are missed and telephone calls are not returned. The impact of your poor performance is severe because it causes me or other staff members to do additional work, and it lessens the respect that supervisors have for you and makes them unwilling to work with you on employee relations matters.

Under the critical element, "Provides Technical Assistance to Managers," the Fully Successful level states, "Provides accurate and timely advice and technical guidance to supervisors on a full range of issues involving discipline, leave, standards of conduct, and procedures for performance-based and adverse actions."

During the opportunity period, you must perform in at least a Fully Successful manner in this critical element. Specifically, you must research the current case law before issuing any draft notice and should use your best judgment to determine the need for research in response to inquiries from managers. This should not cause a great increase in time per case because you have access to a computerized research tool that provides access to MSPB, EEOC, and court decisions and has a very effective search mechanism. For the duration of the opportunity period, you will need to keep a short but concise telephone log of calls and issues to which you respond. During our weekly meeting, we will discuss your responses so that I can review the advice you are providing to supervisors and managers. Additionally, print out a copy of relevant decisions (or case summaries, if that will suffice) that will support your position on the actions for which you are drafting notices. We will review this research each week during our meeting. Over the course of the opportunity period, I expect to find routinely that your advice and notices are accurate, based upon solid and up-to-date research.

I believe that your problems with timeliness can be addressed by a more organized approach to your work. First, you must set reasonable deadlines for accomplishing research and drafting notices. If you know you have several cases where action is pending, do not overcommit yourself to supervisors; come to see me and we will decide whether the work needs to be passed on to

APPENDIX

another staff member. Realistically, notices such as leave restriction memos, reprimands, and proposal notices for the more routine misconduct should be returned to supervisors in draft in 3 working days. More complicated notices should be returned in draft within 5 working days. I recognize that there are always exceptional cases, and I want to work closely with you on establishing deadlines for each of your assignments during the opportunity period. To be determined Fully Successful, you will need to meet established deadlines in 90% of your work. Unless I set a specific date for an assignment, "established deadlines" will be the 3 or 5 working days noted above. During our first weekly meeting, bring a list of everything currently pending on your desk and we will prioritize the work and set deadlines.

Secondly, keeping a telephone log will serve two purposes. The first, as noted above, will give me an understanding of what advice you are giving and will enable me to make recommendations for additional research where necessary. It will also be a way for you to keep records of when you received a call from a manager and when you responded to it. We will review this log at each of our weekly meetings, and I will use it as a method of keeping track of your workload as well as to monitor your progress in becoming more responsive to management inquiries. For the Fully Successful standard, I expect to receive no more than three justified calls during the opportunity period from supervisors complaining that you have not yet returned a call. In order to handle what may be a backlog of unanswered calls, however, I will not count any calls received during the first 2 weeks of this opportunity period.

If you follow the activities outlined above, your performance in the area of providing technical assistance should improve in both accuracy and timeliness. Additionally, I strongly encourage you to discuss cases with me on an informal basis throughout the opportunity period as well as in our scheduled weekly meetings. These meetings will focus on progress made and problems encountered as well as suggestions for improvement in your performance.

[Although this sample involves a non-bargaining unit employee, always be sure to contact your human resources office to determine what agency policies might require you to provide in the way of additional information or referrals for the employee.]

If you believe that a personal, medical, or other problem is causing these performance deficiencies, I encourage you to seek assistance through the agency's Employee Assistance Program (EAP). You can obtain assistance by contacting our EAP contract office at 1-800-555-1212. Participation in this program is voluntary and, with certain restrictions, confidential.

At the completion of the opportunity period, I will make an assessment of your performance. I believe at that time that you will have attained the Fully Successful level in this critical element. You must meet and maintain the Fully Successful level on this critical element for 1 year from the beginning of the opportunity period (the date of this memorandum). Failure to achieve Fully Successful performance on this critical element during the opportunity period or to maintain it during the remainder of the 1-year period may result in removal or reduction in grade without any further opportunity to demonstrate acceptable performance.

APPENDIX

If you have any concerns about this memorandum or require additional guidance on implementing the provisions of it, please let me know as soon as possible. Keep in mind that it is important to refer to the requirements laid out in this notice throughout the opportunity period. Please sign a copy of this memorandum, which serves only to acknowledge your receipt of this notice.

Receipt Acknowledged

_____   _____

Signature   Date

APPENDIX

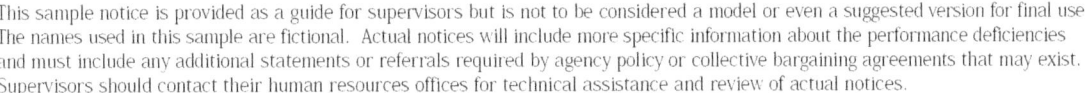

SAMPLE PROPOSAL NOTICE

SUBJECT: PROPOSAL TO REMOVE FOR
         UNACCEPTABLE PERFORMANCE

FROM: MARIA SANCHEZ, CHIEF
         EMPLOYEE RELATIONS DIVISION

TO: JOHN BROOME
         EMPLOYEE RELATIONS SPECIALIST

This is to inform you that I propose to remove you from your position as Employee Relations Specialist, GS-230-13, and from the Federal Service, for unacceptable performance under the provisions of 5 CFR Part 432. This proposal is based upon your unacceptable performance in the following critical element: Providing Technical Assistance to Managers. This action, if taken, will be effected no sooner than thirty (30) calendar days from your receipt of this proposal.

On June 10th, after several months of informal counseling about your performance problems, I issued you a memorandum stating my determination that your performance was at an unacceptable level in the critical element of Providing Technical Assistance to Managers and provided you with an opportunity to demonstrate acceptable performance. Attached you will find a copy of your performance elements and standards as well as the opportunity notice that further clarified your performance standards. During the 90-calendar-day opportunity period (from date _____ to date _____), you failed to achieve the required level of performance in the element listed above. The specific reasons for this proposal follow.

During the opportunity period, I met with you every Thursday with the exception of two dates (July 17th and August 21st) when I was on annual leave and official training, respectively. During those weeks, you were encouraged to contact the Director of Human Resources with any significant cases that came up and I met with you on the Monday following my absences to cover any issues that needed further attention. One purpose of these meetings was for you to demonstrate that you were researching current case law prior to issuing any draft notices to supervisors or providing them with verbal guidance on how to proceed in certain circumstances. As indicated in my summary notes from those weekly meetings (a copy of which you received each week), your performance in this activity was spotty at best. On several occasions, you simply failed to present any research, while at other times you submitted copies of cases dating from the mid-to-late 1980s, which, although relevant to the topic, could not be considered current by any means. I was forced routinely to inform you of specific cases that I knew conveyed the current legal holdings of the Merit Systems Protection Board (MSPB) and the Equal Employment Opportunity Commission (EEOC) that were relevant to the cases you were handling. In several cases this caused rewrites of the draft notices you had prepared, and, in two cases (Montague and Tyrone), you needed to meet with the supervisors and restructure the advice you had given regarding responding to their employees about their appeal rights, if adverse actions were taken against them.

[An actual proposal notice would include more specific examples and documentation of the unacceptable performance.]

By far, the most egregious mistake occurred because you failed to research the current case law on the issue of providing a "firm choice" to alcoholic employees. A supervisor, Dr. Hamlet, presented you with a situation in which an employee with a long history of disciplinary actions associated with his use of alcohol had created a disturbance at work, left work without approval, and remained in an AWOL status for 5 days. You informed the supervisor that no action could be taken at this time because the agency had not given the employee a firm choice between getting medical help for his addiction or facing the consequence of being fired. In fact, the case law on this changed in 1996 when the EEOC and the MSPB found that a firm choice for alcoholics is no longer a requirement and agencies may take actions, including removal for misconduct, even if directly related to the alcoholism. You went on to prepare a notice to the employee providing a firm choice, and, until we reviewed the matter in our weekly meeting of August 28th, you were unaware of the change in the case law. Your failure to properly research resulted in delays in the issuance of an appropriate proposal notice of adverse action to the employee. Additionally, you had to go back to the supervisor and admit that you had given him erroneous advice regarding the need for a firm choice, which he had unfortunately already conveyed to the employee. Clearly, your performance has fallen far short of routinely providing accurate technical advice to the management of this agency, and I find you to be unacceptable in this aspect of your performance.

The second aspect of your performance standard for this critical element involves the timeliness of advice given to supervisors. As I indicated in your notice of an opportunity to improve, I expected you to respond to supervisors in a timely manner by establishing reasonable deadlines for yourself and keeping supervisors apprised of your progress. As an employee at the grade 13 level, I expected you to carry out this assignment with minimal assistance from me. However, I reviewed all of your pending work during our first meeting and established priorities and deadlines for those assignments. Additionally, I asked you to maintain a telephone log for the duration of the opportunity period so I could monitor who was calling and when you were responding to them. On several occasions (dates), when I questioned you, you were unwilling to discuss your own decisions on deadlines for new cases you received during the opportunity period. Finally, as stated in my summary notes from our August 7th meeting, I worked closely with you to set deadlines for all of the work you brought to the meeting. An audit of all of your work submitted during the opportunity period indicates that you met your established deadlines in only 78% of your assignments. This number does not include the three cases (Bottsworth, Carey, and Lucas) where we agreed to extend the deadline due to unusual circumstances beyond your control. Further, I continued to receive a large number of complaints from supervisors that you simply would not return their calls and I was forced to provide them with a status report in the cases where I had that information. Discounting the calls I received during the first 2 weeks of the opportunity period (as stated in the opportunity period notice), I received 12 complaints from supervisors where you were unable to provide me with a supportable reason for your failure to respond to their calls. At this time, I have determined that you continue to be unacceptable under the timeliness aspect of your performance standard.

Conclusion

During the opportunity period, you were given every opportunity to improve to the Fully Successful level but failed to do so. It is my conviction, based on your unacceptable performance, that you are unable to handle all the aspects of the position you hold. Therefore, based on your unacceptable performance in the critical element, Providing Technical Assistance to Managers, as described above, I am proposing your removal from your current position and from the Federal Service.

Request for Reasonable Accommodation

In our weekly meeting on June 26th, you presented medical documentation stating that you were suffering from diabetes and would need accommodation on the job due to your disabling condition. I requested clarification regarding the impact of the diabetes on your ability to work as well as your accommodation request. You responded that you would need sick leave for doctor's visits while you are getting your medication program established and that you would need to store insulin in the agency's health unit and administer that medication once a day. As I stated at the time you submitted this information, I am extremely sorry to hear that you have diabetes, but there didn't appear to be any reason to alter the conditions of the opportunity period except to handle your work myself or assign it to other staff members during your sick leave absences. This was done on each occasion when you were absent, and there were no instances when you were denied use of sick leave.

Additionally, given the brief nature of the absence, I excused your absence without charge to leave each day when you went to the health unit to take your medicine. I have determined that your medical condition has not had any negative impact on your ability to perform because none of the medical documentation you submitted would support that position.

[Always contact your human resources office when an employee raises a medical issue that may be disabling.]

You have the right to respond to this notice both orally and in writing, to prepare and present your response, and to present affidavits of other documentary evidence in support of your response if you elect to make one. You have the right to represent yourself, or to be represented by an attorney or other individual. Designation of your representative must be made in writing to the Human Resources Director within ( ) calendar days of your receipt of this memorandum. You will have ( ) calendar days to present your oral and/or written response to Mr. Taylor, the Assistant Director for Administration. Consideration will be given to extending the ( )-day answer period if you submit a written request to Mr. Taylor stating your reasons for desiring more time. If you

APPENDIX

choose to make an oral reply, either in lieu of or in addition to a written response, you should contact Mr. Taylor and he will schedule an appointment for you to make your response.

You will be allowed a reasonable amount of official time, not to exceed ( ) hours, to review the evidence in support of the reasons advanced in this proposal, and to prepare your written reply. Documentary evidence relied on to substantiate the reason for this proposal is available for your review. Please contact me to if you wish to schedule the use of official time or to review the documentation.

You will receive a written notice of Mr. Taylor's decision as soon as possible after all the evidence in your case, including your written and/or oral reply and all associated documents, has been reviewed and considered. If you do not respond, the decision will be issued after the time allotted for your response has elapsed. If it is determined that your removal is warranted due to an unacceptable level of performance, the decision notice will explain applicable grievance and appeal procedures and how to exercise them.

You will remain in a duty status during the notice period of this memorandum. If you do not understand the reasons given for proposing to remove you, you may contact me for further explanation. Please sign and date the attached copy of this memorandum, which serves only to acknowledge the date on which you received it.

Receipt Acknowledged

_____   _____

Signature   Date

APPENDIX

SAMPLE DECISION NOTICE

SUBJECT: DECISION TO REMOVE FOR
UNACCEPTABLE PERFORMANCE

FROM: BEN TAYLOR, ASSISTANT DIRECTOR
FOR ADMINISTRATION

TO: JOHN BROOME
EMPLOYEE RELATIONS SPECIALIST

In a notice dated and received by you on October 20th, Maria Sanchez, Chief of Employee Relations, proposed to remove you from your position of Employee Relations Specialist, GS-230-13, and from the Federal Service, on the basis of unacceptable performance.

As the deciding official, I have carefully reviewed all the material that formed the basis for the proposal and that was also made available for your review. I have also given full consideration to our meeting of November 2nd, during which you presented your oral response to the proposed removal as well as your written response. While you mentioned several times that you believed I had already made up my mind about this case and that your response was meaningless, you nevertheless challenged, in general terms, the validity of the opportunity period and alluded to many technical inaccuracies. Despite my request that you provide me with a listing of specific errors that occurred in the course of the opportunity period, you never did so. Without any specific information, I cannot give your statements any weight in my considerations. Nonetheless, I have reviewed the documentation for technical inaccuracies and have found none.

You did state that you believed you had a heavier workload than the other specialists in the branch and that it was not possible to keep up with all of the calls from supervisors who needed assistance. However, I have reviewed the monthly case report from your branch and have found that you were assigned approximately the same number of cases to handle as your colleagues during June and July and were given fewer cases, comparatively, during the month of August. Secondly, your cases were not the most complex or arduous available. Although several were complicated, I found nothing of a difficulty that a specialist at the grade 13 level should not be expected to handle. I cannot, therefore, find any justification for your continuing failure to contact supervisors in a timely manner or your failure to meet your assigned deadlines. The evidence in the proposal notice and evidence file clearly indicates that you failed to meet the requirements for Fully Successful performance regarding the timeliness of your work.

You did not specifically respond to the issue of your failure to provide accurate technical guidance to supervisors and managers. I find the evidence compelling that your supervisor attempted to give you a mechanism for reviewing current case law and ensuring that your advice reflected any and all recent changes in the law. It is also obvious that, in many cases, you did not conduct appropriate research prior to advising managers and drafting notices that had to be revised or completely redone based on poor preparation on your part.

Your response dealt with the issue of "blame" for cited errors or delays; you felt you were being blamed for actions that were not your fault. The real issue is not one of blame but of responsibility; the examples cited by your supervisor clearly indicate that you have too frequently not met your responsibilities and have shown no indication of improvement or even of particular concern. While you have demonstrated an ability to perform this job in the past, you are currently failing to carry out one of the key functions and responsibilities of the position, and have made no effort to improve in this respect.

[An actual decision notice will discuss all pertinent issues raised by the employee in the response. Deciding officials may need to look into statements in the response or appoint a factfinder to determine the validity of some statements.]

I have very carefully reviewed your allegations of disability discrimination based on your medical documentation, including the diagnosis of diabetes. Although you did not inform your supervisor of this condition until 2 weeks into the opportunity period, I concur with the assessment by Ms. Sanchez that your medical condition did not impact on your performance and that there was no need to alter the conditions of the opportunity period. Memoranda of counseling reflect that your work was handled by coworkers or by your supervisor on any day that you were on sick leave for doctor's visits. I have reviewed your statements regarding your supervisor's negative attitude toward you after you revealed your condition. However, the examples you cite are of your supervisor's counseling you concerning errors in your work or criticizing your failure to research appropriately. These reactions from Ms. Sanchez are typical of any supervisor reviewing an employee's work during an opportunity period and I cannot find any evidence of a discriminatory motive. Nor can I find anything to support your argument that the opportunity period should have been discontinued until you got your medical situation under control.

I find that all the instances of unacceptable performance specified in the proposal notice of October 20th are sustained and that your performance in the critical element, Providing Technical Assistance to Managers, failed to meet the Fully Successful standard, as clarified in the opportunity period notice you received from Ms. Sanchez. I also find that you were given a reasonable opportunity to demonstrate acceptable performance, but failed to do so. Therefore, I find that your removal for unacceptable performance is warranted.

Accordingly, it is my decision that you be removed from your position of Employee Relations Specialist, GS-230-13, and from the Federal Service, effective November 30th. You will be continued in an active duty status with pay until the effective date of this action.

Because you have raised the argument that your medical condition, diabetes, prevented you from working in your position, I am notifying you of your option to file a request for disability retirement with the U.S. Office of Personnel Management. Should you wish additional information on how to submit this application for retirement, please contact Ms. Sarah Gloucester at (202) 555-1212.

APPENDIX

Disability retirement applications must be filed within 1 year of your last day of employment (November 30th).

Additionally, in accordance with Title 5 USC 4303 and 7121(e) and (f), you have the right to appeal this action to the Merit Systems Protection Board (MSPB), Washington Regional Office, 5203 Leesburg Pike, Suite 1109, Falls Church, VA 22041. You will be deemed to have exercised your option at such time as you timely file a notice of appeal to the Board.

An appeal to the Board must be in writing and must contain the information required by MSPB regulations, a copy of which is attached. You may submit an appeal at any time after the effective date of this action, November 30th, but not later than thirty (30) calendar days after that date. A copy of the appeal form that you may use is also attached. Please sign and date the attached copy of this memorandum, which serves only to acknowledge the date on which you received it.

[Note that this sample involves a non-bargaining unit employee who would not have grievance rights under a collective bargaining agreement. It is essential that you obtain information from the human resources office regarding appropriate appeal and/or grievance rights.]

Additionally, because you have alleged that this action was discriminatory based on your medical condition, I am informing you of your right to file a complaint with the agency's Office of Equal Employment Opportunity (EEO). You may elect to file an appeal with the MSPB or to file a complaint with the EEO office, but you may not elect both at the same time.

You may bring any questions you have about this removal to me and I will explain any points that are unclear to you. If you have questions about your rights or the procedures used in this matter, you may contact Mr. Garrett Johnson, Director of Human Resources.

Receipt Acknowledged

_____   _____

Signature   Date